JAPANESE
EMPLOYER—
AMERICAN
EMPLOYEE

JAPANESE EMPLOYER— AMERICAN EMPLOYEE

✦

An Employee Career Survival Guidebook

Sam S. Bowman EE, MBA, CPIM

iUniverse, Inc.
New York Lincoln Shanghai

JAPANESE EMPLOYER—AMERICAN EMPLOYEE
An Employee Career Survival Guidebook

iUniverse books may be ordered through booksellers or by contacting:

iUniverse
2021 Pine Lake Road, Suite 100
Lincoln, NE 68512
www.iuniverse.com
1-800-Authors (1-800-288-4677)

ISBN-13: 978-0-595-37462-5 (pbk)
ISBN-13: 978-0-595-81856-3 (ebk)
ISBN-10: 0-595-37462-X (pbk)
ISBN-10: 0-595-81856-0 (ebk)

Printed in the United States of America

This book is dedicated to my wife,
Elizabeth Ann (Bitsy) Bowman, who
lived it with me and understands.

Contents

INTRODUCTION

An American employee may face major, career-jeopardizing problems when working for a Japanese organization. In the six chapters of this book, I categorize these problems, their primary causes, and my recommended solutions.

It is intended to be a survival guide to help American employees of Japanese organizations save their careers.

This book is based upon my four-year experience as such an employee in the United States and Japan. In addition to my personal experience, I drew upon numerous interviews that I conducted with American employees of six Japanese automotive original equipment manufacturers in the United States, as well as with American employees of second-tier Japanese suppliers to my employer.

I was a salaried employee when I worked for the Japanese, but what I learned should apply, in most instances, to all Americans who work for Japanese employers.

It is my sincere wish that my experience might facilitate a mutually beneficial working relationship between the American employee and the Japanese organization.

The six chapters of this book cover the following common problems:

Chapter 1: Unusually High Conflict
Chapter 2: Business Decision Making
Chapter 3: Organizational Structure
Chapter 4: Teaming
Chapter 5: The Language Barrier
Chapter 6: Job Security

By defining the primary causes of these six major problems and recommending solutions to them, I offer a unique career aid to the struggling American employee.

Will American employees face other problems while working for a Japanese organization? Yes, they will, but what I have presented should give them the means with which to save their careers.

American female employees will face these same problems. They must also carry an additional burden. Japanese managers have a difficult time accepting a female in a leadership function. The recommended solution to each of the major problems discussed in this book will certainly help women save their careers, but they must also enhance the recommended solutions if they are to overcome this additional barrier.

Please forgive me for using the masculine pronouns *he* and *his* in this book. Be assured that what I have written applies to both genders, but for ease of reading, I have stayed with the masculine.

I sincerely hope that what I have written will accomplish my objective in aiding both the American worker and the Japanese organization without offending either. To the extent that I describe problems and solutions that may be offensive to either or both groups, I apologize. To offend is certainly not my intent; however, candid definition and presentation is required to aid both groups in recognizing and resolving their problems. To do otherwise would benefit neither.

1

UNUSUALLY HIGH CONFLICT

Problem Statement: The American salaried employee, working in either a wholly owned Japanese company or an American/Japanese joint venture, will inevitably experience an unusually high level of conflict.

Primary Cause: Cultural differences

Areas of Conflict and Recommended Solutions:

A. Management style: Objective vs. Subjective

The American employee is trained to perform under a specific job description with specific goals and objectives that are to be accomplished over a defined time period. Periodic performance progress reports from superiors are expected. Wage increases and/or promotions depend upon successfully meeting these goals and objectives within the required time frame.

Japanese superiors do not think in such specific terms. As a means of trying to satisfy American expectations, they may attempt to operate in this mode by agreeing (even in writing) to specific goals and objectives plus the required performance time frame, but they don't really mean what they say.

This is not an intentional attempt to confuse or mislead the American employee. The Japanese simply cannot operate in this narrow per-

1

spective. They have been trained to work cross-functionally as necessary to meet the goals of the company. Flexibility is ingrained in their psyche, and they expect their American subordinates to operate in this same manner, regardless of what goals and objectives have been established in writing. It is easy for the American employee to become confused and misunderstand what is expected.

Let me illustrate this problem with a personal experience. I first encountered this type of conflict when a new executive vice president of my American/Japanese employer, an automotive component manufacturing company, arrived from Japan. I was materials manager and reported to that executive vice president. My previous Japanese boss had been in the United States for the normal five-year tour. His five years of experience working with Americans, plus his sincere desire to make the company successful, allowed him to work within the traditional American method better than any other Japanese executive that I have met.

Timing was such that establishing annual goals and objectives for the work force was an initial task of the new executive vice president. I dutifully submitted my aggressive and challenging recommendations for what I would like to accomplish over the next year. The time frame for these goals and objectives was included in my recommendations.

The new executive vice president and his boss, the company president, who was an American, reviewed my recommendations. After this extensive review process, the new executive vice president gave written approval of my recommendations.

As the year progressed, I had periodic performance reviews with my Japanese boss. These critiques stated that I was on target to accomplish what I had set out to do; however, they had little meaning. When I had my annual performance review, I was criticized in writing for not being flexible in my interdepartmental actions. I received what I considered to be a fair merit increase, but the "flexibility" criticism bothered me. I asked my Japanese boss why this problem was just now being brought to my attention, because I had not heard it in the interim reviews.

I stated that I also felt that his criticism was incorrect because major progress had been made in reducing the interdepartmental functional barriers that normally exist within most American companies. Generally, these barriers exist within American companies because of functional checks and balances among interrelated departments. For example, the finance department checks inventory levels controlled by the materials department, the materials department checks the production output of the manufacturing department; et cetera.

In our joint-venture Japanese/American company, all department heads had praised each other for attaining significant functional cooperation while still maintaining their checks-and-balances responsibilities. How could he arrive at this criticism? His only response was that, in his opinion, my effort had not been at the level that he wanted to see, so the criticism would stand.

The company president had signed my performance review, effectively approving the criticism, so I went to discuss the issue with him. He stated that he had to appease his Japanese subordinates to a certain extent, even though he did not agree with the criticism. He also stated that he was trying to maintain a harmonious working relationship with the executive vice president; therefore, he had approved my performance review with the criticism intact. He also stated that I should not worry about the criticism because other department heads had received essentially the same feedback, but he knew that there was really no merit to any of it.

Since the president of the company was not truly in support of my Japanese superior's criticism, I disregarded the matter. Boy, was I wrong! I later learned the bitter lesson of subjective Japanese performance requirements. In the eyes of the Japanese boss, what he gives his employee in writing does not matter. What matters to the Japanese boss is how he subjectively values the employee.

Recommended Solution:

Do it both ways. Respond to both the American goal-oriented performance expectations and the Japanese subjective, flexible ones. Keep using the written goals and objectives technique to meet the requirements of American management, but recognize that the Japanese don't evaluate you through this method. The Japanese demand subjective, functional flexibility. Consider departmental responsibilities and territories very fluidly. You must be recognized as a general problem solver operating across all departmental boundaries. You must use *both* methods—a difficult but not impossible task.

B. Work vs. Family

American workers expect to be able to discuss both business problems and personal problems affecting their job performance with their superiors. At a minimum, they expect their superiors will offer a sympathetic ear. At a maximum, they expect to receive some near-term recommended solutions to their problems. The American boss will normally discuss both types of problems. The Japanese boss is much more restrictive. In general, the Japanese believe that discussions of personal problems on company time are inappropriate. Work accomplishment takes top priority. When pushed to respond, the Japanese boss has a strong tendency to look at employees' "immediate response desires" as typical American brusqueness. On rare occasions, Japanese bosses will discuss personal and work-related problems with American employees, but their recommended solution (reflecting their true feelings regarding the problem) will most likely not come out of that discussion. Therefore, this is the wrong approach to follow with the Japanese boss.

What path must the American employee follow to resolve his problems? The Japanese problem-solving technique is after-hours socializing, where the formalities of the office are much less strict. In this environment, the Japanese superior recognizes the unwritten law of being able to "tell is like it is" because they can always save face and mitigate embarrassment by saying they had too much to drink. Having participated in many of these sessions, I can testify that most Japanese business executives use after-hours socializing to relieve work-related stress. The work barriers are down, and business and personal conversation flows freely. It is a good time to communicate.

I don't mean that it is necessary to join in heavy partying. Simply being on hand to enter into informal conversations will do much to overcome communication problems. Of course, the American employee must be invited to "join the club." A forced-entry approach will be severely rebuffed.

Unfortunately, after-hours socializing faces another culture conflict. Americans expect to do their work, with overtime as required to get the job satisfactorily completed, then return to their families. Most strive to achieve some level of balance between work life and family life. This is not the Japanese way. Work comes first with the Japanese. Other Japanese family members understand and expect this type of priority.[1] If the American employee wants to succeed in his job, he should try to shift the work/family balance to accommodate this socializing. No, it's not an easy adjustment for either the employee or his family, but it is a cost associated with this career path.

There are other important aspects of after-hours socializing that the American must understand. This time is also used by the Japanese to help them develop understanding and trust regarding their Japanese peers and subordinates. I have observed this same technique applied to Americans who participate. The Japanese focus on understanding the psychological makeup of American employees rather than their formalized job performance. A Japanese executive must determine whether he

---

1. There is some belief that Japanese wives become Americanized when they accompany their husbands to the United States, causing them to demand less work time and more family time. This apparent liberation movement gives great comfort to American wives; however, having seen and spoken to wives of Japanese executives after their return to Japan, it is my opinion that the success of their "emancipation" effort has been overstated.

can trust an American not to cause embarrassment, both as an employee and as an individual. Such determinations are an important result of this social time.

Americans should note that even with all the personal benefits of this socializing technique, it is taboo to *directly* address business or personal matters during this social time. You must be very subtle in any discussion. It's a paradox. This is the time for the American employee to have business or personal discussions with his Japanese boss, but he can't directly initiate these discussions. The discussion must be mixed within the social activity in a non-offensive manner. If answers to work-related problems emerge, I have found that the Japanese generally will honor these answers; however, it will be up to the employee to interpret these answers correctly. It takes some practice.

An example of the success offered by this social/business interchange involved the location of a piece of welding equipment used in the manufacturing process. The American manufacturing manager and I had been trying for two weeks to get our Japanese boss to approve the physical layout that we had proposed but we had been unsuccessful. The subject came up during a socializing event under a Japanese initiated discussion of "process improvements". My Japanese boss proposed basically our layout plan as though it was his idea. The manufacturing manager and I were quick to agree and subsequently acted even quicker in implementation. By both of us hearing the layout approval, we felt that there was little risk in taking quick action. My Japanese boss did not change his mind. It is doubtful that we would have gotten Japanese approval by the standard formal route since we would have never thought to make it a Japanese idea.

The business direction of the company can also be clarified during this time. It's hard to believe, but very true, that such important issues as business direction and problem resolution can occur during after-hours social time, but that's the Japanese way.

In many Japanese organizations in the United States, Americans have rebuffed Japanese attempts to include them in their "after-hours office." This affront has caused the Japanese to continue the practice only with their Japanese business associates. This avenue of communication and understanding is so important to conflict prevention and resolution that I strongly recommend that the American employee participate. Don't hesitate to join this activity when invited. You have too much to gain, career wise.

Recommended Solution:

Make after-hours socializing a part of your job. Explain this requirement to your family. They probably won't like it, but it may be more welcome than loss of your job.

C. The Human Resources Void

The majority of the employees in a Japanese company operating in the United States will be American; therefore, an American normally will occupy the top position in the human resources (HR) area. American employees have traditionally looked to HR to represent them and their problems to upper management.

It is worth noting that, in my opinion, American salaried employees are today given a poorer level of support by HR than hourly employees. Corporate downsizing, resulting in consolidation of most HR activities at higher levels in the organizational structure, has left many on-site HR staffs so thin that they must concentrate on problems of the hourly employee at the expense of representing the salaried employee. Salaried employees many times end up with a "1-800" number to support them in their HR problems.

Inject this basic lack of HR support for the salaried employee into a Japanese company, and the support void is enlarged. In fact, I have seen some instances where local HR has made an already bad working situation worse. How can this happen? In all fairness, American HR leaders are not sufficiently trained to handle the differences between objective (American) and subjective (Japanese) management philosophies. I'm not saying that local HR management doesn't attempt to resolve the problems of salaried workers. Many times they do, but because they are ill-equipped to solve problems caused by the underlying philosophical differences, they have little chance to help the American salaried employee.

Can HR make the situation worse? Yes, they can. A salaried employee who is trying to deal with the HR support void may be very confused as to what HR responsibilities he must manage on his own. If he asks local HR for assistance in resolving a business problem related to Japanese management, and local HR accepts the assignment, the American salaried employee will go back to work and allow HR to do their job. However, he should not rely on HR to fully solve the problem. Human resources in such an enterprise typically neither understands the Japanese way nor has sufficient time to pursue a solution. Realistically, the problem can even be made worse at this point. The American salaried employee, thinking that perhaps Japanese management will understand his position through the advocacy of HR, will continue with business as usual. This means he may continue making the same mistakes (in the eyes of his Japanese managers). His problem will continue to grow.

Local HR has some responsibility to support the American salaried employee in resolving his problems with Japanese management, but HR really can't do the job alone. The only successful problem resolution that I have achieved by taking the HR path occurred when HR and I jointly presented the problem to Japanese management. I don't mean that we held a three-way meeting. Rather, after I met with HR and we agreed on a unified approach to the problem at hand, HR discussed the problem with Japanese management in a separate meeting. I later compared notes with HR to see whether we got the same answer from management.

It was necessary to make certain that there was no misinterpretation of either the problem or the response. If the answers agreed, then I was on fairly safe ground to believe that the problem had been correctly understood. If I didn't like the Japanese solution to the problem, I would work again with HR until I was either satisfied with the solution or realized that I would not get the solution that I desired. By using this method, I at least had third-party (HR) confirmation of the answers given by Japanese management. Obviously, we didn't use this method too often because it was very time-consuming and because I couldn't get the local HR department to allocate much time to it.

Recommended Solution:

Don't assume that the local HR managers can help you. You must solve the problem yourself, even though you may, at times, get some support from HR by coordinating your efforts.

2

BUSINESS DECISION MAKING

Problem: The American employee has a difficult time adjusting to the Japanese business decision process.

Primary Cause: Differences in business decision-making methodology.

Areas of Conflict and Recommended Solutions:

A. Timing

It is infuriating to the American employee that it takes so long for Japanese executives to make a business decision. To the American, the meticulous, analytical detail followed by the Japanese in making a business decision looks like a waste of time. The real difference in time perception between the two cultures is the crux of the problem.

The American business decision sequence is as follows:

1. Analysis—as much as is needed to arrive at a decision.

2. Implementation.

3. In-process adjustment as necessary.

By contrast, the Japanese must avoid the risk of making a mistake to prevent embarrassment. Therefore, extensive, painstaking front-end analysis, with hours of discussion, is used to support a decision that will require no adjustment and, thus, no embarrassment. Once the decision is made, implementation is relatively quick.

Interestingly enough, the total time from conception to success may be the same using either method. Time *perception* is where cultural differences occur.

Following the Japanese decision-making process may lead to missed business opportunities if the required commitment point falls too early in the decision-making time frame. The Japanese look at such lost business opportunities philosophically—we missed one chance, but another will come along. Remember that from the Japanese perspective, it is better to miss a business opportunity than to make a mistake. There must be no embarrassment.

Recommended Solution:

Americans must understand and learn to respect the Japanese decision methodology. If the Japanese don't mind missing an opportunity, then neither should the Americans. Just relax. Fighting this particular battle is futile.

B. The Decision Path

Consistent with these timing differences between Japanese and American methods is a difference in the decision path. The American path is from top to bottom, whereas the Japanese path is from bottom to top. Remember, avoiding embarrassment is the Japanese's top priority. Consensus that a business decision is correct must be reached within the organization before it is implemented. To reach this consensus, the focus is on those who must implement the decision.

Today, most successful American business executives arrive at the best choice by consulting with those who will be most affected by a particular decision. This is certainly an improvement over the older, totally autocratic system; however, the final decision still comes from the top. The Japanese work extensively with every level in the organization that will be affected by the decision. If those who will be most affected by the change can't guarantee successful implementation, the proposed change will be dropped.

Recommended Solution:

Recognize that the Japanese bottom-to-top decision path has the primary objective of avoiding mistakes and thus preventing embarrassment. Prevention of embarrassment will often override a decision to implement what an American believes is a sound business decision.

C. Blocking

When Japanese managers oppose implementation of an American-proposed business improvement, they do not directly state their opposition nor debate the issue. Instead, they masterfully employ the "analysis paralysis" and "delay" techniques. Here is a real-life example of this strategy.

My employer's American management wished to authorize a change designed to reduce costs in the manufacturing process used by one of our major suppliers. Because our product was an automotive safety component, the supplier performed extensive analysis and testing of the change to ensure it met the requirements established by our American design and quality control engineers. The supplier's new process had already been successfully implemented at one of our American-owned sister companies. Field performance data from that company verified that the change met our design and quality requirements.

Since this change would yield several hundred thousand dollars in annual cost savings, the Americans wanted to authorize the change. The Japanese managers controlled product design, but since their area of control did not officially extend to changes so deep within our supplier's process, the change authorization could be given by our American quality control and design management. Receiving the blessing of the design management in Japan would have been preferable, but it was not mandatory.

As we approached our target date to authorize our supplier to make the process change, more and more technical questions started coming in from the Japanese design department. Out of a spirit of cooperation, we provided answers to every question, but more questions kept coming. It became obvious that the Japanese were unofficially rejecting the change through the "analysis paralysis" process. To implement the change, local management would have had to override the implied rejection by Japan. This could have been done but wasn't. A significant cost reduction was lost.

Japanese also block business decisions through delay tactics. An example of this occurred in an electronic data interchange (EDI) improvement project. Approximately 10 percent of our raw material components had to be imported from Japan because we had found no United States suppliers who were able to meet our technical specifications. We placed weekly material orders for these components with our Japanese parent via lengthy fax transmissions. Transmission legibility was a continuing problem. To eliminate this problem, American management suggested that we use EDI technology in our import order processing.

We placed weekly orders via EDI to our American suppliers, so we knew that this method gave excellent legibility and was cost effective. Therefore, we thought our proposal to extend the process to our Japanese parent was sound. We also thought they liked the idea.

To this end, a Japanese/American project team was established. An American international EDI communication carrier was selected. On a trip to Japan, I hand-carried an EDI software package that was compatible with both the American and Japanese computer operating systems. Software installation took place, and transmission testing was next on the implementation agenda. Then the delays started. Connectivity problems on the Japanese end were officially blamed for these delays. This was hard to believe because I had attended meetings in

Japan in which potential connectivity problems were discussed and resolved in the typically thorough Japanese manner. Also, our EDI communications carrier assured me that they had this same type of international data link in place in their own office in Japan, and it was operating successfully. Connectivity was not the real problem. The American members of the project team tried repeatedly to find out the reason for the delay, but there was nothing but a wall of silence from the Japanese. We never did learn the reason for the Japanese opposition; however, the delay tactic worked well. The project was dropped.

Recommended Solution:

Although Japanese blocking tactics may frustrate you, don't fight them. More opportunities will come along.

3

ORGANIZATIONAL STRUCTURE

Problem Statement: The Japanese organizational structure is not what it seems.

Primary Cause: The Japanese organizational structure is fluid—not fixed—until fluidity doesn't work.

Areas of Conflict:

The Japanese concept of organizational structure comes from the same roots as their job description philosophy. The organizational structure may be outlined on paper (like it is in America), but it is fluid in its execution. American employees have difficulty in adjusting to a fluid organizational structure and become even more confused when the fluid structure becomes a fixed one. This generally happens when the fluid structure causes a problem.

Many American companies are moving toward a less formal organizational structure through the team-based process. (This process will be discussed in more detail later.)

Experience has taught us that management responsibility and control must still be maintained to a large extent. You can't delegate total authority and responsibility to teams, or chaos will reign. A formal organizational structure and chain of command reporting should still be maintained to make the teaming process effective.

Most American employees have gained their business experience within a fixed organizational structure and see this structure as reinforcing their specific job responsibilities. Departmental barriers have been broken to a great extent through teaming. This has been a good step, but each department still has specific responsibilities. It is difficult for the American employee to know how much cross-departmental responsibility to assume. Misunderstanding and conflict grow from this confusion.

Remember that the Japanese organizational philosophy demands heavy cross-functional activity with little regard to how responsibilities are defined on paper. Once again, an American employee working for a Japanese employer can find himself in operational never-never land.

Let me illustrate this point with another experience. When I was materials manager in an American/Japanese joint venture company, one of my areas of responsibility was shop floor control of production. Our company had implemented the highly cost-effective Japanese Kanban[1] shop floor control technique with a significant level of success. However, we still needed to fully implement the true ("pull") Kanban process flow used by the Japanese. Our interim-type Kanban had a fairly high level of "push," based upon both actual and forecasted customer orders. Attaining true "pull" Kanban was what we wanted to accomplish next in the implementation process.

Having studied books and articles on the "pull" Kanban process, I was technically knowledgeable but still lacked hands-on operating experience. To gain this experience, I was sent to Japan to be trained by my counterparts in one of our Japanese partner plants. The training I received was thorough and practical.

Upon returning to the United States, I was full of enthusiasm and energy to move the company up to true "pull" Kanban performance. However, I found that in my absence a cross-functional total quality

---

1.   "Kanban, Just-In-Time At Toyota", Edited by the Japan Management Association, Translated by David J. Lu, English translation copyright © 1986 by Productivity, Inc., Productivity Press, Stamford, Connecticut

(TQ) team of system users and support personnel had been formed to implement the "pull" Kanban technology. I was listed only as the process owner in the team structure. This designation meant I had little direct participation in the TQ team's activity.

I believed I was still responsible for communicating my newly gained knowledge to the team, so I dutifully attended the initial team meetings. When I attempted to help the team with my knowledge, I was told by my Japanese superior (the new executive vice president) that the TQ team of users and support personnel needed to arrive at their own solution to the installation problem without benefit of my direct help. Yes, this was the Japanese way of letting the solution come from the users, or at least appear to come from the users. My department had official responsibility for the success of the "pull" Kanban shop floor operation, but I, the department head, was not to lead the installation directly.

At that time, I didn't sufficiently understand the Japanese methodology of subtle direction and fluid organizational structure. I was confused by this approach, so I followed my Japanese superior's direction to let the TQ team arrive at the solution.

Several weeks passed, and the TQ team made little progress on the installation. The "pull" Kanban installation team looked to my Japanese superior for guidance because he was very familiar with the process and would break his own non-interference rules to try to bring some progress about. I didn't like the lack of progress, so I attempted to subtly assist in the team's installation efforts by giving suggestions to team members outside of their normal TQ meeting. However, this subtle approach was not successful.

After a few more weeks of floundering around by the installation team, my Japanese superior called me to his office and severely criticized me for not contributing to the success of this installation. I was absolutely dumbfounded. I reviewed with him the sequence of events that led me to adopt a somewhat hands-off attitude regarding this project.

A. My thorough Kanban training in Japan.

B. My enthusiastic desire to install this capability.

C. Because I was trained, and by an American definition, it was my responsibility to ensure a successful installation.

D. A cross-functional TQ team of users and support personnel had been formed to do the installation and no leadership role was assigned to me.

E. My direct participation in the activity of the team was expressly prohibited at my supervisor's direction.

He acknowledged that I had correctly stated the scenario, but said he still believed I had not done my job. Because I wasn't clear on how I had failed, I continued to push for further definition of what he thought I should have done. (Pushing for an immediate answer was a mistake; see "Work vs. Family.") After much prodding, he told me that I should have realized that there was a problem with the installation (I told him that I did) and that I should have taken control of the team even though I had been told not to do so. At this point I finally saw how the fluid Japanese organizational structure—in this case the cross-functional TQ team—reverts to the American fixed departmental structure when the fluid structure doesn't work. Responsibility for successful completion of the project silently returned to me when project failure was imminent. This also was symptomatic of Japanese management's tendency to do anything they can to disassociate themselves from failure.

Recommended Solution:

Recognize that the Japanese have a fluid organizational structure until it doesn't work. At that time, the fixed structure, with corresponding fixed responsibilities, automatically kicks in to correct the problem. Be sensitive to this when organizational crossover needs to take place, and be flexible enough to make the change. Remember, if you had responsibility under the fixed organizational structure, it might ultimately be yours again even if you have been told otherwise.

4

TEAMING

Problem Statement: The dynamic American employee has difficulty functioning within the team-based operating environment, but the Japanese mislead you into believing that they expect business problems to be resolved via this method.

Primary Cause: Differences in leadership concepts. Japanese managers do not desire dynamic leadership from their American employees.

Areas of Conflict:

The American team-based adaptation of the Japanese "quality circle" concept can yield some amazing improvements in productivity and problem-solving within the hourly work force. I confess that, at first, I had my doubts that positive results could be attained. I feared that this was just another corporate fad that would flame up at top management level and then pass into oblivion once the novelty wore off.

At first it was difficult to establish the makeup of the teams within the hourly work force. However, we didn't make the common mistake of trying to "empower" the teams with too much management responsibility.

The first teams were too large, which limited individual participation. Also, too much emphasis was placed on solving major problems. It took too long to obtain good results, thus discouraging the team members.

Instability of team membership was another serious problem that had to be overcome. Shifting work assignments kept the teams in constant turmoil. Good results were minimal. Management finally recognized that team stability had to be considered before team membership assignment was finalized. Temporary membership reassignments could be better tolerated by a team when it knew that the reassigned member would be returning. Of course, some permanent reassignments were necessary, but they were intentionally minimized.

Once these deficiencies were recognized, teams were reduced in size, were better aligned with daily work assignments (cells), and were made more stable. Additionally, the scope of team problem solving was reduced to those problems directly under the control of the team. By narrowing the scope of responsibility, solutions could be more quickly achieved by the team.

This was when productivity improvements really started to occur, and I became a believer in the validity of the teaming concept within the hourly work force.

Salaried employees contributed to the hourly workers' success by acting either as team coaches or in a resource support capacity. The team coach's primary responsibilities were to keep the team focused on solving a defined problem and to call for outside support from other salaried personnel (in other departments) as required. As I said, this concept worked surprisingly well within the hourly work force; however, the team-based concept fell apart within the salaried ranks.

What was the problem? Remember my earlier example of the TQ team formed to install the "pull" Kanban process? Knowledgeable salaried employees were not allowed to exercise their leadership ability. The Japanese preferred team-based problem solving despite the risk of possibly not arriving at a solution at all. Failure to achieve a specific solution to a problem was acceptable to the Japanese as long as it was not considered by their upper management to be a personal failure on their part. They did not want the knowledgeable, dynamic Americans to express their leadership ability. The individual was not to stand out from the team. It is very challenging for an American with proven leadership ability to change his style and conform to the group methodology. Strong American leaders have great difficulty accepting that arriving at a correct solution through the team process justifies the difficulties encountered within that process.

Another revelatory aspect of teaming was how the Japanese can use this technique to achieve the solutions that they desire. I became aware that when team-based action was taken in areas of special concern, our Japanese management predetermined what outcome they desired, but took great care to try to make the solution appear to come from the team. Japanese management subtly rejected team recommendations in those areas until the team arrived at the Japanese desired solution.

Of course, this manipulation contaminated the teaming process. When our salaried American employees became aware of it, a strong negative backlash occurred. The teaming process was downgraded in the minds of many of the American salaried employees.

However, it is unfair to condemn an entire process because impure aspects are contained within the process. Remember that Japanese management will retreat from the teaming process if the team's failure to arrive at an acceptable solution has the potential to cause the managers personal embarrassment. Some manipulation of the process occurs in response to this fear.

In my years of American business experience, I have yet to find any process, procedure, or theory that remains pure once it encounters the realities of human intervention in actual application. American and Japanese business cultures are indistinguishable from this standpoint. The important thing to look at is whether there is a generally realized benefit, rather than dismissing the process due to limited areas of impurity.

Recommended Solution:

Recognize that, in general, the team-based process works well at the hourly employee level. At the salaried level, however, a leader must learn to lead through the team—not around it—if the process is to have a chance of success. Additionally, be aware that the team-based process has impurities that must be overlooked if one is to appreciate the real benefits of the process.

5

THE LANGUAGE BARRIER

Problem Statement: Neither the American employee nor the transplanted Japanese executive has been well-prepared to overcome the language barrier. The language barrier greatly hinders the organization's chances of operational success by creating misunderstanding and confusion.

Primary Cause: Japanese companies assume that the six years of English required in the Japanese educational system are sufficient to ensure good verbal and written communication with American employees. This is a misconception. Even when tutoring in English is provided to the Japanese executive prior to his departure for a United States assignment, it is insufficient. Another problem is that Americans believe responsibility to bridge the language barrier rests solely with the Japanese.

Areas of Conflict:

Communication difficulties create problems in any organization, but they can be extremely troublesome within a transplanted Japanese organization. It is fairly obvious how the Japanese/English language barrier negatively affects each of the problems previously identified in this book.

Translation of Japanese sentence structure into English can create great confusion. Elementary examples of this situation are: "Yes, I don't want to do that," and "No, I do want to do that." Correct interpretation of what the Japanese speaker is trying to convey is indeed difficult.

Please understand that in defining this problem it is necessary to speak in generalities. My experience is that this is a problem with a majority of Japanese executives assigned to work in the United States. Of course, there are exceptions. Most of the exceptions are found within the ranks of younger Japanese executives who have had more exposure to English, and specifically to idiomatic American English. These younger executives have been helpful in correcting and preventing some misunderstanding, but the language barrier still remains.

It is especially unfortunate when a language problem exists at the senior executive level. At that level great damage can occur. To illustrate, the new executive vice president that I mentioned in Chapter 1 could barely speak English. His predecessor was very fluent in our language, so adjusting to this new manager was extremely difficult. Meetings were longer and more tedious than normal because of the need to translate almost every sentence. Even so, nobody really knew if the executive vice president understood the outcome of the meeting. Individual meetings with him were extremely frustrating, producing more confusion than clarity. American employees made a concerted effort to avoid meeting with him.

It finally became necessary for our company president to direct the executive vice president to receive outside tutoring in English. Of course, this was kept very quiet, but the word got around. I know that it caused him much embarrassment, especially among his Japanese business acquaintances outside our company and his Japanese subordinates within our company.

This individual had a high level of pride, so he did not accept the tutoring directive easily. It was obvious that he resisted it, because even after a considerable period of time, there was not much improvement in his English. It continued to be such an obstacle that the company's performance was adversely affected.

Not much later, management announced that this individual would be returning to Japan at the end of his initial three-year work period. This was highly unusual because the normal tour of duty for Japanese executives was five years—the first three-year period plus a two-year extension. His early return severely strained the relations between our joint venture partners.

This example of what can happen in a Japanese/American company as a result of the language barrier is an extreme one, but I have also seen the same problem to a lesser degree cause other operating difficulties. The language barrier is real. The American employee working in this environment will be faced with a difficult situation that must be recognized and resolved.

Recommended Solution:

One obvious solution is for the Japanese to improve the English language training given those executives selected to work in the United States.

One solution can be implemented by the American employee either with or without the help of his employer. Learn to speak and understand Japanese. It's really not as far-fetched as it seems. My company held some voluntary after-hours training in Japanese. It was taught by an English-fluent, lower-level Japanese executive. Because it was informal, work requirements began to interfere with the training sessions and the training sessions eventually ended. Even though it was a short-lived course, we Americans who attended the sessions significantly improved our Japanese language skills.

I strongly recommend that the American employee who wants to succeed within a Japanese organization learn Japanese, either through an education program provided by their company or on their own initiative. It must be a formal training program. The informal approach will fail due to work priorities.

I must add another comment within this recommended solution. Japanese executives have told me that they get very tired of conducting business in English. These same executives responded very well to my limited conversational ability in Japanese (gained in our informal class). Becoming reasonably fluent in Japanese management's language offers a great opportunity to turn a normally adversarial relationship into one of great support. Do it! It's your career we're talking about.

6

JOB SECURITY

Problem Statement: The American employee can be misled into believing that there is more job security within a Japanese organization transplanted to the United States than there is in an American organization. For most American employees, this increased job security is basically a myth.

Problem Cause: Job security in Japan has been well-advertised. It is logical for the American employee to think the same situation would apply to Japanese organizations in the United States.

Areas of Conflict:

Lifetime employment for the Japanese worker has been a well-publicized characteristic of Japanese industry. (Current Japanese economic realities have significantly eroded this principle.) The price that the Japanese worker pays for this job security—extreme loyalty, dedication, and obedience to the company—is certainly known in the United States; however, it is so difficult for the individualistic American employee to follow this work philosophy. Sincerely trying but being unable to achieve the Japanese expected work ethic has led many American employees to approach their work with a false sense of security. Increased job security for the American salaried employee does not exist within the Japanese organization unless the employee convinces management that he is willing to pay their price.

As I stated earlier, most Japanese companies operating in the United States have an American leading the HR operation. American HR pol-

28

icies and procedures have been implemented so that United States labor law requirements are fulfilled. Most experienced American employees are familiar with these fairly standard policies and procedures, but they become confused when Japanese distortion is applied. Here is an example of what I observed relative to this issue.

An American salaried employee working for a transplanted Japanese organization was performing well below the minimum American job standard. This employee was smart enough to project a strong but false image of job dedication to Japanese top management. To obtain improvement in this employee's job performance, an American-type corrective action procedure, authorized by both the American HR manager and Japanese top management, was implemented. (It was necessary for the employee's immediate supervisor to give extra support to the HR manager regarding this personnel problem.) The employee received personal counseling from his immediate American superior. His areas of deficiency were clearly enumerated and discussed. Outside training was authorized to try to correct the problems. Corrective action plans with specific time frames were clearly defined. More frequent performance reviews were held to keep the individual aware of his progress along the corrective action path. However, his job performance did not improve significantly.

A verbal warning was given and documented during the initial performance reviews, but because of the lack of improvement over the established corrective-action time frame, a written warning was also issued to the individual. His poor job performance continued. It was necessary to issue a second written warning. Again, his poor job performance continued. Termination of the employee was agreed to by both his immediate American superior and the HR manager, but when this final action was presented to the responsible Japanese executive for approval, he asked if this procedure could be avoided by finding the employee a less responsible position within the company. (This Japanese executive had been part of all the earlier counseling and outside training decisions regarding the employee.) Yes, this low-performing individual had fooled Japanese management into believing that he was paying their price for being an employee! The Americans could see the deception, but the Japanese could not.

The employee's immediate American superior and the HR manager were totally frustrated with the Japanese executive. They pointed out that the company's own rules would not allow them to demote the nonperforming employee and bring in someone to do his critical job assignment. At this point, all of the Japanese management got involved in the issue. They counter-proposed shifting more of the nonperforming employee's work to one of his peers so that his work could be accomplished without having to terminate him. The unfairness of heaping extra work on a good employee to cover for a nonperforming employee was pointed out to Japanese management. They did back off this official position, but still got their way by default through not allowing the termination of the nonperforming employee. He kept his job because he could play the employment game by Japanese rules.

The morale of the American salaried work force took a nosedive. This was especially true for the nonperforming employee's American supervisor and the HR manager. Most of the American salaried employees were striving to make the company succeed. The company was small enough that they were all aware of the poor job performance of one individual. They also could recognize when standard American corrective action activities were used relative to that individual. When he still was not terminated, the inability of Japanese management to correct an adverse employee problem was visible to all. There were many who felt that the Japanese were not fair or impartial in their dealings with the American salaried workforce. At a minimum, the American salaried employees were confused as to what personnel policy applied to them. It appeared that the way to retain job security was to play the Japanese game; however, most of these employees were ill-equipped to follow this course. The Japanese retained their favored employee, but the total cost to the company for this action was much more than they realized.

In the previous example, Japanese management unfairly rewarded a nonperforming employee who knew how to play their game. What about the American salaried employee who does his job well, has no performance problems, but does not play the game by the Japanese rules? This employee is much more vulnerable from a job security standpoint. I am in no way saying that high-performing American salaried employees who fail to project the correct image to the Japanese will automatically lose their jobs. What I am saying is that this type of salaried employee is in a higher job risk category.

I believe that every corporate employee plays the political game to some extent, either consciously or subconsciously. Some play it much better than others. The Japanese do not have a corner on the market here. Advancement within the American corporation depends quite a lot on how well the individual employee can play the game. What confuses American employees of transplanted Japanese corporations is the difference in ground rules between American and Japanese corporate politics. Playing corporate politics at the low level necessary to succeed within an American company will most likely bring failure within a Japanese company. Within a Japanese company, one's image of loyalty must be extremely visible and recognized by all Japanese management.

Why does an American salaried employee who is doing a good job in a Japanese company, who has no performance problems, and who plays the political game in a way that would bring promotion and success within an American corporation, have higher job risk? It is because this type of employee is most likely to be misled by his Japanese superiors.

Remember that the Japanese must profess to support the American HR policy with regard to their American salaried employees. They don't really believe in American personnel management policies and procedures, but they must pretend to follow American rules while in this country. They hold the standard American performance reviews and evaluations, but their underlying desire is not to have any one-on-one confrontations with their American salaried subordinates. This leads to false performance evaluations that mislead American salaried employees into thinking that their jobs are secure.

There have been many documented instances where American salaried employees have received great and glowing performance reviews from their Japanese superiors, only to find themselves terminated shortly thereafter. Many of these dismissals have led to litigation, which is an unfortunate situation for both the employee and the Japanese company. What can the American salaried employee do to achieve the maximum level of job security while working for Japanese employers?

Recommended Solution:

The most effective way for an American salaried employee to have job security within a Japanese organization in the United States is to learn to play the political game at the Japanese level. Don't directly and openly challenge the Japanese way of business operation. Continuously make them aware of all that you do for the company using their business methodology. You must make Japanese management believe that you are a true member of their team. Those who cannot do this should at least be aware that all those excellent evaluations that they receive from Japanese superiors do not mean what they say. Protect yourself!

SUMMARY

Let's review the major problems faced by American employees working in United States outposts of Japanese organizations and what can be done to handle these problems.

UNUSUALLY HIGH CONFLICT

Primary Cause: Cultural differences
Areas of Conflict and Recommended Solutions:

A. Management Style: Objective vs. Subjective

Recommended Solution: Perform your job following both American (objective) and Japanese (subjective) management styles.

B. Work vs. Family

Recommended Solution: Make after-hours socializing part of your job. This solution will require a great deal of understanding from your family.

C. The Human Resources (HR) Void

Recommended Solution: Don't assume that the local Human Resources (HR) management can help you. You must solve the problem yourself, even though you may, at times, get some support out of HR.

BUSINESS DECISION MAKING

Primary Cause: Differences in decision-making methodology
Business Decision Making Problems and Recommended Solutions:

A. Timing

Recommended Solution: Understand and learn to respect the Japanese business decision methodology. If the Japanese don't mind missing a business opportunity, then neither should you.

B. The Decision Path

Recommended Solution: Recognize that the Japanese bottom-to-top decision path has the primary objective of avoiding mistakes and preventing embarrassment. Prevention of embarrassment will override a decision to implement what an American believes is a sound business opportunity. Don't fight this Japanese business technique.

C. Blocking

Recommended Solution: Although frustration is a normal result of the blocking tactic, don't get uptight. Another opportunity will come along.

ORGANIZATIONAL STRUCTURE

Primary Cause: The organizational structure is fluid—not fixed—until fluidity causes problems.

Recommended Solution: Recognize that the Japanese have a fluid organizational structure until it creates problems. To avoid any failure-related embarrassment, the Japanese will change to the American fixed structure without any prior warning. Be sensitive to when this organizational crossover takes place and be flexible enough to make the change.

TEAMING

Primary Cause: Difference in leadership concepts. Dynamic leadership from American employees is not desired by the Japanese.

Recommended Solution: Recognize that, in general, the teaming process works well at the hourly level. At the salaried level, the dynamic American salaried employee must learn to lead through the team and not go around it. Also, be aware that the team-based process has impurities that must be overlooked if one is to gain the real benefits of the process.

THE LANGUAGE BARRIER

Primary Cause: Japanese do not give sufficient English-language preparation to the executives they send to the United States. Americans rely solely on the Japanese to make the language transition.

Recommended Solution: The Japanese must improve English-language training of their executives prior to sending them to work in this country. American salaried employees can greatly contribute to the resolution of this problem as well as improve their career advancement chances by learning to speak and understand Japanese.

JOB SECURITY

Primary Cause: American salaried employees assume that the job security rules applied within industry in Japan also apply in the United States.

Recommended Solution: Learn to play the political game at the level expected by the Japanese. Those who cannot do this must at least be aware that they must make extra efforts to protect their jobs.

CONCLUSION

The presence of Japanese-owned and Japanese-American joint venture organizations in this country is a recognized fact. In my opinion, for the foreseeable future, not only will these organizations remain here, but others will be added to their numbers. As long as these organizations operate in this country, there will be a need for American employees to staff them.

Can an American employee find a successful career within a Japanese organization? I believe that he can, but he must be willing to pay a price for a successful career that is greater than that demanded by American organizations. As long as this higher price is recognized and accepted by the American employee, then both the American employee and the Japanese organization will benefit from the association.

Those American employees who are either working for Japanese organizations or who are contemplating employment with a Japanese organization and are not willing to pay the price of success should seriously consider another career choice. There is enough stress in working for an American organization. Very few American employees can stand the greater stress level found within a Japanese organization operating in this country. It's just not worth it.

As an American employee, if you chose to make your career within a transplanted Japanese organization, it is my sincere hope that this guidebook will assist you in making your career a success. Good luck!

978-0-595-37462-5
0-595-37462-X

www.ingramcontent.com/pod-product-compliance
Lightning Source LLC
Chambersburg PA
CBHW021046180526
45163CB00005B/2306